Eli   *y*
M   at
Aberystwyth University, then in 1983 became a
trainee journalist with the *Birmingham Post and
Mail.* She has continued to work in journalism,
mainly in a freelance capacity. At first, she special-
ized in writing about sport, but since 1990 has
turned her hand to other subjects, including
eating disorders, travel, women's issues and
contemporary Christianity.

100 Ways
TO PRAY MORE
EFFECTIVELY

Elizabeth Filleul

Marshall Pickering
An Imprint of HarperCollinsPublishers

Marshall Pickering is an Imprint of
HarperCollins*Religious*
Part of HarperCollins*Publishers*
77–85 Fulham Palace Road, London W6 8JB

First published in Great Britain
in 1995 by Marshall Pickering

1   3   5   7   9   10   8   6   4   2

Copyright in this compilation © 1995 Elizabeth Filleul

Elizabeth Filleul asserts the moral right to be
identified as the compiler of this work

A catalogue record for this book is
available from the British Library

ISBN 0 557 02965-X

Printed and bound in Great Britain by
Woolnough Bookbinding Limited,
Irthlingborough, Northamptonshire

Introduction

'Have you ever observed that we pay much more attention to a wise passage when it is quoted than when we read it in the original author?' This observation – by Philip G. Hamerton in *The Intellectual Life* – is undoubtedly true. Sometimes wise sayings or comments can go unnoticed in a lengthy text, but placed on a page of their own in an anthology they can be much more thought-provoking, even life-changing.

100 Ways to Pray More Effectively is just such an anthology, but with a difference. It is intended for the Christian wishing to deepen their relationship with God; for those seeking to converse with God more often and to listen to what he is saying in return. The essential element to achieving all this is prayer.

But what exactly *is* prayer? According to the *Oxford Encyclopaedic Dictionary*, it is 'a solemn request or thanksgiving to God'. The *BBC English Dictionary* defines praying as 'speaking to God in order to give thanks or ask for help'. While it is true that, for many people, prayer is little more than a 'shopping list' of requests to God – 'Look after Mum, Dad and the cat, and help me get promoted at work' – there is more to prayer than that. It can also be much deeper and more satisfying and exciting than simply asking for help. Here are some examples of what effective prayer can entail:

- Prayer is praising God for the wonders of his creation.

- Prayer is allowing God to work in his own time, and not setting limits on him.

- Prayer is talking intimately to God about your concerns, without having to explain every intricate detail.

- Prayer is taking note of what God says to you, and remembering it throughout the day.

- Prayer is telling God how much you love him.

- Prayer is taking a long walk alone with God, telling him your concerns along the way.

- Prayer is enjoying laughter and sharing sorrow.

- Prayer is singing a hymn of praise as you go about your daily tasks.

- Prayer is thanking God for all the things in life which you appreciate and enjoy.

- Prayer is placing yourself at the heart of another person's situation, by interceding for them.

During Jesus' earthly ministry, prayer was the only thing the disciples asked him to teach them about. We too need to learn how to pray, and how to create a two-way relationship with God through prayer. Down the centuries spiritual leaders, teachers and writers have shared with us their insights into prayer. Many of their suggestions appear in this book. I urge you to go on to read their work, and unearth even more ways of deepening your relationship with God.

The selected quotations show tremendous variety in strategies for praying more effectively. They cover places to pray, ways to pray and prayers to pray. I have my personal favourites; you will too. What will become clear is that there is no single suggestion which will be appropriate for every individual at any one time. Our circumstances are different and *we* are different. Also, God approaches and responds to us as individuals.

Each quotation is accompanied by a suggestion for reflection or practical action. Sometimes there are suggestions of people, places or concerns you might pray for. Occasionally the suggestion takes the form of a question, inviting you to consider the adequacy and benefits of your prayer life – to God and to yourself.

This book is not the definitive guide to an instant, perfect prayer life. The Christian's relationship with God is not like that. But, by following the advice, you will find yourself thinking more deeply about the time you spend with God and about the prayers themselves.

Finally, for prayer to be *really* effective, every

Christian needs to start viewing the world and its concerns through the eyes of God. I hope that some of the insights given by the quotations in this book will enable the reader to begin to do just that.

Put God at the centre

A preacher related how, one night, he bowed his head in silent prayer before delivering a sermon and prayed, 'O God, help me.' The reply he says he got from God was this: 'I will do better, I will use you.' He said, 'That amendment was decidedly better. I was asking God to help me – *I* was the centre. I was calling God in for my purposes. But "I will use you" meant I was not at the centre; something beyond me was the centre, and I was the instrument of a purpose beyond myself. God's answer shifted the whole centre of gravity of my prayer.'

SELWYN HUGHES, CWR Prayer Diary

🕭 Ask God to be at the centre of your life and to use you in whichever way he wants.

Don't worry if you're tired

DOG-tiredness is such a lovely prayer, really, if only we would recognize it as such. Sometimes I hear, 'I'm so dog-tired when I get to chapel, I can't pray.' But what does it matter? We don't matter. Our Lord can pray just as well through a dog-tired body and mind as through a well-rested one, better perhaps. It is the same with pain and suffering of all kinds. Our advance guard on the infirmary wing could tell us that.

MOTHER MARIBEL OF WANTAGE

🐾 When you feel too tired to pray coherently, remind yourself that physical fatigue is no obstacle to the Lord.

FATHER, hear the prayer we offer:
Not for ease that prayer shall be,
But for strength that we may ever
Live our lives courageously.

L. M. WILLIS

❧ Next time you pray, don't ask God to make your
life easier. Ask him for the strength to face
problems and difficulties.

Praise God for daily life

I thank you for anything which happened to me today which made me feel that life is really and truly worth living.

I thank you for all the laughter that was in today.

I thank you, too, for any moment in which I saw the seriousness and the meaning of life.

I thank you especially for those I love, and for those who love me, and for all the difference it has made to me to know them, and for all the happiness it brings to me to be with them ....

WILLIAM BARCLAY

🐾 At the end of today, make a list of all the good things that have happened, the laughter you have shared, and any insights about life which you received. Praise God for all of them.

HOLY obedience to the insights, the concerns that come, that persist, and are in accord with co-operation with God's way of life is not only the active side of prayer, but it is the only adequate preparation for future prayer.

DOUGLAS V. STEERE, *Prayer and Worship*

🔖 As you pray today, make a note of the things that lead from your prayers – the concerns God brings to your mind. Bring those concerns before the Lord again before you go to bed.

Check out people's happiness

BEFORE we passionately wish for anything, we should carefully examine the happiness of its possessor.

Duc de la Rochefoucauld

🌿 What sort of things have you been praying for lately? Think of people who already possess them. Are they happy? Are they content? If not, maybe you are asking God for the wrong things.

Thank God for your favourite things

FOR sausages, baked beans and crisps
For papers full of fish and chips
For ice cream full of chocolate bits
Thanks, God.
For furry caterpillars to keep
For wood-lice with their tickly feet
For crabs we watch with bits of meat
Thanks, God.
For bicycles and roller skates
For playing football with my mates
For times when I can stay up late
Thanks, God.

CANON DOBSON, *Prayabout*

🐚 List some of your favourite things – foods, activities, animals, people – and thank God for them.

Pray in secret

AND whenever you pray, do not be like the hypocrites; for they love to stand and pray in the synagogues and at the street corners, so that they may be seen by others. Truly I tell you, they have received their reward. But whenever you pray, go into your room and shut the door and pray to your Father who is in secret; and your Father who sees in secret will reward you.

MATTHEW 6:5–6

❧ Learn the habit of saying simple prayers in the middle of busy situations – in the supermarket, in a queue, in a business meeting. Praying quietly, inwardly, will not draw attention – except from God.

JESUS' life was a life of obedience. He was always listening to the Father, always attentive to his voice, always alert for his directions. Jesus was 'all ear'. That is true prayer: being 'all ear' for God. The core of all prayer is indeed listening, obediently standing in the presence of God.

HENRI J. M. NOUWEN, *Making All Things New*

🐾 Today, read of the gospels and see how Jesus was always listening to his Father.

Take regular exercise

HEALTHY prayer necessitates frequent experiences of the common, earthy, run-of-the-mill variety. Like walks and talks and good wholesome laughter. Like work in the yard, and chit-chat with the neighbours, and washing windows. Like loving our spouse and playing with our kids and working with our colleagues. To be spiritually fit to scale the Himalayas of the spirit we need regular exercise in the hills and valleys of ordinary life.

RICHARD FOSTER, *Prayer*

🦶 Set aside some time today for talking to the neighbours, going for a walk, doing the garden or playing with your children. Let these experiences inform your prayer.

Recognizing your spiritual stage

THERE are two sorts of prayer: the one tender, delightful, loving and full of emotions; the other obscure, dry, desolate, tempted and darksome. The first is of Beginners, the second of Proficients who are in the progress to perfection. God gives the first to gain souls, the second to purify them.

MIGUEL DE MOLINOS, *The Spiritual Life*

&amp#128075; Which stage in your prayer life do you feel you're at? Ask God to help you be ready to move on to the next one.

God isn't a bell-boy!

GOD is not a cosmic bell-boy for whom we can press a button to get things.

H. E. FOSDICK

❧ Apologize to God for all those times you have regarded him as a 'cosmic bell-boy'. Promise that from now on your will will be to do his will.

Praise God for unanswered prayers

I have lived to thank God that all my prayers have not been answered.

JEAN INGELOW

🐾 Make a list of prayers which you are now glad God didn't answer. Make another list, of blessings from God which you didn't ask for. Think about those things you have recently been asking God for – if those prayers are not answered, will you perhaps one day be grateful?

Be ready to listen

GIVE to us, O Lord, that quietness of mind in which we can hear you speaking to us, for your own name's sake.

Lord, you have taught us in your word that there is a time to speak and a time to keep silence.
As we thank you for the power of speech we pray for the grace of silence.

Make us as ready to listen as we are to talk,
ready to listen to your voice in the quietness of our hearts and ready to listen to other people who need a sympathetic ear.

Show us when to open our mouths and when to hold our peace that we may glorify you both in speech and in silence through Jesus Christ our Lord.
FRANK COLQUHOUN

🐾 Spend some time today quietly before God, just listening to what he has to say.

I remember reading years ago a little tract written by Frank Laubach, a great man of prayer, in which he described one of his prayer practices. When he is on a journey, even on a streetcar going a few blocks, he tries to spot somebody on the car who seems to him to be in distress, or perhaps just tired or lonely, and to direct his prayers toward that person as though the divine possession were streaming out of him to this other person.

H. L. PUXLEY,
International Journal of Parapsychology

🌢 The next time you travel by bus, train, boat or plane, look around at your fellow passengers. Choose someone to pray for and ask God to bless them.

Pray out of faith, not insecurity

WHAT we often do is throw ourselves on our knees and say, 'Give us work, give us money, give us employment, give us, give us, give us.' And actually that is not the prayer of faith, that is the prayer of insecurity. The prayer of faith is what Jesus said to his Father: 'Not my will, but yours be done.'

DAVID SUCHET

❧ Are your prayers those of faith or of insecurity? Ask God to help you pray from faith.

EARLY on in my prayer pursuit, I heard a wise maxim: 'Pray as you can, not as you can't.' In other words, pray and listen to God in a manner which holds meaning for you personally. Beware of falling into the trap of aping another person's prayer style. For the would-be listener to God, this advice is priceless.

JOYCE HUGGETT, *Listening to God*

  Which style of prayer seems to bring you closer to God? Decide to use it all the time, rather than trying to adopt someone else's. Pray as you can, not as you can't.

Pray for a safe journey

BLESS to me, O God,
The earth beneath my foot,
Bless to me, O God,
The path whereon I go;
Bless to me, O God,
The thing of my desire;
Thou evermore of evermore;
Bless thou to me my rest.

Bless to me the thing
Whereon is set my mind,
Bless to me the thing
Whereon is set my love;
Bless to me the thing
Whereon is set my hope;
O thou King of kings,
Bless thou to me mine eye!
CELTIC JOURNEY BLESSING

🐾 As you set out on a journey today, if only to the
shops or to work, pray this prayer.

Don't forget God after worship

Yoᴜ let me not when [this] morning prayer is said, think my worship ended and spend the day in forgetfulness of you.

Rather from these moments of quietness let light go forth, and joy and power, that will remain with me through all the hours of the day;

Keeping me chaste in thought;

Keeping me temperate and truthful in speech;

Keeping me faithful and diligent in my work;

Keeping me humble in my estimation of myself;

Keeping me honourable and generous in my dealings with others;

Keeping me loyal to every hallowed memory of the past;

Keeping me mindful of my eternal destiny as a child of yours.

Through Jesus Christ my Lord.

Jᴏʜɴ Bᴀɪʟʟɪᴇ, *A Diary of Private Prayer*

🍂 Choose one of the things Baillie mentions in his prayer – e.g. being chaste in thought, faithful and diligent at work – and make it your priority today.

Pray for orphans

PLEASE, Lord, bless all the children who don't have a mother or father – and those who may even have no family at all. You know what they are feeling and how much love they need. Father, you love us all. Give more love than ever to these children now. Heal their hurts and ease their pain. In Jesus' name. Amen.
CAROL WATSON

🐾 Ask God's blessing on all orphans. Think particularly of street children in countries like Brazil. Donate time, money or clothing to a charity which helps orphans.

A generous prayer is never in vain.

ROBERT LOUIS STEVENSON

❧ Pray that relatives and friends should find their heart's desire. Remember, generosity of spirit is a key New Testament theme and often requires that we put others' needs or wishes above our own.

Be silent

Before Prayer

I weave a silence on my lips … my mind … my heart.
Calm me, O Lord,
as you stilled the storm.
Still me, O Lord,
keep me from harm.
Let all the tumult
within me cease.
Enfold me, Lord,
in your peace ….
DAVID ADAM, *The Badge of Glory*

🐾 Spend some time in silence, shutting your troubles
firmly from your mind. Relax in the Lord's presence.

I was hungry,
    and you formed a humanities group to discuss my
    hunger.
I was imprisoned,
    and you crept off quietly to your chapel and prayed
    for my release.
I was naked,
    and in your mind you debated the morality of my
    appearance.
I was sick,
    and you knelt and thanked God for your health.
I was homeless,
    and you preached to me of the spiritual shelter of
    the love of God.
I was lonely,
    and you left me alone to pray for me.
You seem so holy, so close to God
But I am still very hungry – and lonely – and cold.

ANONYMOUS, *handed in to a Shelter regional office*

❦ When you pray about someone else's situation,
    think of a way you can meet their need with
    practical action. Then go out and do it.

Light a fire!

'**O!**' says one person, 'if we had another minister. O! If we had another kind of worship. O! If we had a different sort of preaching.' You do not need new ways or new people, you need life in what you have. If you want to move a train, you don't need a new engine, or even ten engines – you need to light a fire and get the steam up in the engine you now have!

It is not a new person or a new plan, but the life of God *in them* that the Church needs. Let us ask God for it! Perhaps he is ready to shake the world at its very foundations. Perhaps even now he is about to pour forth a mighty influence upon his people which shall make the Church in this age as vital as it ever was in any age that has passed.

CHARLES SPURGEON,
Spiritual Revival, the Want of the Church

🍂 Ask God to reignite you so as to fulfil the potential which exists in you. Then pray that you will use your new-found fire to reignite others too.

WATCH over one another in gentleness and tenderness. Know that we cannot help one another out of a snare of our own strength, for only the Lord, who must be waited upon, can do this in all and for all.

ISAAC PENINGTON, *Letters on Spiritual Virtues*

🐌 As you pray for other people, remember you personally may not be able to help them – trust God to do that. But where you can help, be ready to do as God tells you.

Let prayer be first and last

BEGIN now, as you read these words, as you sit in your chair, to offer your whole selves, utterly and in joyful abandon, in quiet, glad surrender to him who is within. In secret ejaculations of praise, turn in humble wonder to the Light, faint though it may be. Keep contact with the outer world of sense and meanings. Here is no discipline in absent-mindedness. Walk and talk, and work and laugh with your friends. But behind the scenes, keep up the life of simple prayer and inward worship. Let inward prayer be your last act before you fall asleep and the first act when you awake.

THOMAS KELLY, *A Testament of Devotion*

🔖 This week, let prayer be the first thing you do when you wake up, and the last thing before you go to sleep.

Ask God to bless your home

GOD bless the house
From site to stay,
From beam to wall,
From end to end,
From ridge to basement,
From balk to roof-tree,
From found to summit,
Found and summit.

CELTIC PRAYER

🐚 Ask God to bless every corner of your house – and
let it be God's house, to use the way he wants.

Pray for the homeless

WHEN you sit happy in your own fair house,
Remember all poor men that are abroad,
Eternal dwelling in the house of God.
ALCUIN OF YORK

🔖 Sit in your favourite room or chair, and thank God
for your home. Pray for everyone who is homeless.
Pray that governments in all countries should seek to
put a roof over all citizens' heads.

I<small>T</small> is surprising how tempting it is to ignore the opportunity to pray when it does arise. In the mornings I often have a chance to be alone with God while the children are at school. But the breakfast dishes need washing up and then I must hoover downstairs, put the washing machine on and go shopping. It is a real struggle to let go of all this for a moment and sit down and pray, while I'm looking at the cornflakes stuck to the sides of the cereal bowls. I am pulled in two directions. I long to have a space to pray, but I also long to leap up and wash the dishes. If I do succumb to the lure of the kitchen (which is never strong at other times) it is fatal. As soon as I've finished washing the last spoon, you can guarantee that the doorbell will ring and my time with God will be lost altogether.

A<small>NGELA</small> A<small>SHWIN</small>, *A Tapestry of Voices*

Decide on the most convenient time of day to talk to God and make a note of it in your diary. Keep the date.

Talk to the Father

BY praying, you deepen your relationship with Jesus. But prayer is not just asking for things. Prayer is being with him, sharing things with him. God is almighty. He does know everything. He is in full control and he loves you and cares for you very deeply. Just as a human father likes to hear all that his children have been doing during the day, so our heavenly Father loves to hear all we do – all our hopes and joys, our fears and worries.
NORMAN WARREN, *What's the Point?*

🐦 Tonight, before you go to bed, address God as 'Father' and tell him what you've been doing today.

WHAT is prayer? In short, it is a dialogue with God in which our attitudes and thoughts are grafted into God's thoughts. If we are to pray effectively, we must condition our thoughts to divine thoughts, and our attitudes must be right in relation to God's. Whether or not our right thoughts are actually verbalized, they are a savoury offering pleasing to God. But how can we judge whether or not our thoughts are right in God's eyes? Our standard of measure is the word of God.

PAUL YONGGI CHO, *Praying with Jesus*

❧ What has been preoccupying your thoughts lately? What does the Bible have to say about the subject matter? Check that your thoughts are in line with God's.

Accept everyone as equal

I F this is God's world, there are no unimportant people.

GEORGE THOMAS (LORD TONYPANDY)

🍃 Think of people on the periphery of your life, who you never pray for. Pray for them now, knowing they are as important to God as those you pray for daily.

BUT if we are to look for everything from God, all our good thoughts and feelings, how is it that we are often so dull and indifferent, satisfied to say our prayers coldly and without any preparation? Why do others try so hard to inflame their imagination as if prayer depended on their own efforts, as if it were not necessary that God's action should govern and direct their prayer? Since prayer is a supernatural act, we must earnestly ask God to produce it in us, and then we must perform it tranquilly under his guidance.

JEAN-NICHOLAS GROU, *How To Pray*

❧ Remember that prayer does not depend upon your own efforts alone. Ask the Holy Spirit to guide you in prayer.

Pray for world leaders

PLEASE guide the leaders of many different countries at the meetings where they try, by working together, to make the world a better and a safer place. Help them to want peace rather than power, and show them how they can share the food in the world that no one need be hungry.

BERYL BYE, *Please, God*

🔖 Pray for the leader of your country and for another world leader. Pray that they should want to see God's will fulfilled in the world and in the countries they govern.

To business that we love we rise betime,
And go to't with delight.

WILLIAM SHAKESPEARE, *Antony and Cleopatra*

Which hobby or activity is most likely to get you out of bed early? Praise God for it – and ask him to help you enjoy prayer as much, or more.

Thank God for pets

WE give thanks for domestic animals. Those creatures who can trust us enough to come close. Those creatures who can trust us enough to be true to themselves.

They approach us from the wild. They approach us from the inner world. They bring beauty and joy, comfort and peace.

For this miracle, and for the lesson of this miracle, we give thanks. Amen.

MICHAEL LEUNIG, *Common Prayer Collection*

🐾 Praise God for the companionship of your pet, or the pet of someone you know.

Make prayer envelopes

A<small>T</small> last I have found a way of prayer that is not excruciatingly boring or meaningless, or hopelessly fragmented. On the desk in front of me … lies a pile of about thirty long brown envelopes. On the outside of each is written one or more names. Inside each sealed envelope is a written prayer for the people concerned. Each day I pick up the envelope, hold it up to God, and ask him to do whatever is needed for them.

ADRIAN PLASS,
The Growing Up Pains of Adrian Plass

ﷺ Write on envelopes the names of those people you regularly pray for. Inside, write down specific prayer requests. In time, you will see how those prayers come to be answered. Remember to thank God for answering those prayers.

Put God first

O Lord, help us to put you first; others next;
and ourselves last, now and always.
The Infant Teacher's Prayer Book

🐾 Do something today which involves putting God
first, others next and yourself last. Reflect on the
results of your action and resolve to repeat
the exercise tomorrow.

PRAISED be our Lord for the wind and the rain,
For clouds, for dew and the air;
For the rainbow set in the sky above
Most precious and kind and fair.
For all these things tell the love of our Lord,
The love that is everywhere.

ELIZABETH GOUDGE

☙ Thank God for today's weather. Resolve never to
complain about the weather he sends.

Express adoration

IN adoration we enjoy God. We ask nothing except to
be near him. We want nothing except that we would
like to give him all. Out of this kind of prayer comes the
cry 'Holy! Holy! Holy!' In this school of adoration the
soul learns why the approach to every other goal had
left it restless.

DOUGLAS V. STEERE, *Prayer and Worship*

❧ Spend time in prayer, telling God how much you
love and worship him.

ADMITTANCE to the school of prayer is by an entrance test with only two questions. The first one is: Are you in real need? The second is: Do you admit that you are helpless to handle that need?

Whatever I have learned about prayer has come as the result of times when I could answer a resounding *yes* to both questions. Looking back over my life, those times of need stand out like mountain peaks rather than, as we might suppose, valleys of despond. Peaks – because each time I learned something important about God – how real he is and how gloriously able to answer prayer.

CATHERINE MARSHALL, *Adventures in Prayer*

What have been the 'peaks' in your spiritual life? Spend some time reflecting upon them and on what you learnt.

Sing a hymn to God

TAKE my voice and let me sing
Always, only, for my king;
Take my lips, and let them be
Filled with messages from thee.
FRANCES RIDLEY HAVERGAL

🔔 Sing a hymn or worship song to God. If you can,
create a worship song of your own.

T H E kingdom of heaven may be compared to someone who sowed good wheat in his field; but while everybody was asleep, an enemy came and sowed weeds among the wheat, and then went away. So when the plants came up and bore grain, then the weeds appeared as well. And the slaves of the householder came and said to him, 'Master, did you not sow good wheat in your field? Where, then, did these weeds come from?' He answered, 'An enemy has done this.' The slaves said to him, 'Then do you want us to go and gather them?' But he replied, 'No; for in gathering the weeds you would uproot the wheat along with them. Let both of them grow together until the harvest; and at harvest time I will tell the reapers, "Collect the weeds first and collect them into bundles to be burned, but gather the wheat into my barn."'

MATTHEW 13:24–30

• Think about any 'weeds' God hasn't yet removed from your life. Would uprooting them have harmed the 'wheat'?

Bless your loved ones

G O D bless all those that I love;
God bless all those that love me;
God bless all those that love those that I love
And all those that love those that love me.

NEW ENGLAND SAMPLER

Think of yourself in the centre of a web, and how
large the web becomes when those who love you,
those who love them, and those who love those who
love you are added. Though you cannot name them
individually, ask his blessing on each of them.

Learn from all Christian traditions

WITH prayer, we are entering holy ground, and we simply must confess our poverty of spirit. No single denomination, or church, or group of people contains so much of the truth on this matter that it can succeed while isolating itself from the rest of the Christian community. We need the wealth of experiences and hard-won insights of all who are seeking to follow Christ and become his friend.

RICHARD FOSTER, *Devotional Classics*

This coming Sunday, visit a church of a different denomination to your own and see what you can learn from them about praying to and worshipping God.

Laugh

GIVE us a sense of humour, Lord, and also things to laugh about. Give us the grace to take a joke against ourselves and to see the funny side of the things we do. Save us from annoyance, bad temper, resentfulness against our friends. Help us to laugh, even in the face of trouble.

A. G. BULLIVANT

🐚 Invite some friends around to watch a comedy programme or video. Praise God for the talents of the writers and actors, and thank God for the joy you find in friends and laughter.

Cry

JESUS, you wept over Lazarus your friend and over Jerusalem your city, and we too are deeply saddened by personal tragedy and international disaster.

Show us how we can weep with those who weep so that we can come alongside others in their darkness rather than judging them for their faults, as you have done with us and for us in the Father's name.

FURTHER EVERYDAY PRAYERS

🐾 The next time you are moved to tears, by personal or international tragedy, pray about your sadness. Remember that Jesus cried too and understands your sorrow.

Take a prayer walk

GOD of all our cities,
Each alley, street and square,
Pray look down on every house
And bless the people there.

JOAN GALE THOMAS, *God of All Things*

🍂 Take a prayer walk around your locality, asking God's blessing on each household. Pray specifically for those whose individual circumstances and needs you know.

O Lord, thou knowest how busy I must be this day; if I forget thee, do not forget me; for Christ's sake.

GENERAL LORD ASHLEY

When you're busy, God may be far away from your thoughts. Do you think you are ever far from his? Praise him for his constancy.

Care for animals

HEAR our humble prayer, O God, for our friends the animals, especially for animals who are suffering; for any that are hunted or lost or deserted or frightened or hungry; for all that must be put to death. We entreat for them all thy mercy and pity and for those who deal with them we ask a heart of compassion, gentle hands and kindly words. Make us ourselves to be true friends to animals and so to share the blessing of the merciful.

ALBERT SCHWEITZER

🐾 Join an animal welfare organization, and pray for their work.

REMEMBER, Lord, all the infants, the children, the young, the middle-aged, and the elderly who are hungry, sick, thirsty, naked, captive or friendless in this world. Be with those who are tempted with suicide, those who are sick in soul, those who are in despair.

Remember those who are in prison, all those who are under sentence of death. Remember the widows and widowers, the orphans, and those who travel in a foreign land. Remember all who this day will work under oppressive conditions. Amen.

LANCELOT ANDREWES, *Private Devotions*

  Pray for the world's needy and especially anyone you know personally who is suffering.

Read the Bible first

GEORGE Müller, that great man of prayer, claimed that for many years he was defeated in his prayer life because he had not understood the importance of meditating in the word before approaching God in prayer. When you learn this lesson and take time to read God's word prior to prayer, you do what the pilot does when he tunes up his engine in preparation for a flight. The word starts your thinking, your aspirations, going in the right direction. This prepares you to pray prayers that can be answered, for they will be prayers that are aligned with the will of God, and where the will of God is done, there the power of God can come.

SELWYN HUGHES, *CWR Prayer Diary*

🐾 Before you pray, read a passage from the Bible. Meditate upon it, asking God to direct your thoughts.

Pray for those who pray

ANYONE who lives, prays. Anyone who possesses human life possesses a deeper spiritual life as well, and the journey of prayer is nothing more nor less than a gradual awakening to the reality of recognizing what is already there.

DELIA SMITH, *A Journey into God*

🐦 Pray for those who pray only in a crisis – when someone is ill, as their plane is about to take off, in a natural disaster. Ask that, through their prayers, they may want to know who they are praying to.

Ignore short cuts

I N the spiritual life, there are no tricks and no short cuts. Those who imagine that they can discover spiritual gimmicks and put them to work for themselves usually ignore God's will and his grace. They are self-confident and even self-complacent. They make up their minds that they are going to attain to this or that and try to write their own ticket in the life of contemplation.

T HOMAS M ERTON, *Contemplative Prayer*

🐾 Have you ever used 'spiritual gimmicks' to try to influence God or to prove to other Christians how holy you are? Resolve never to use short cuts again, but to concentrate on finding out God's true will for your life.

POUR forth, O Christ, your love upon this land today.
ANONYMOUS

❧ Pray for your country. Pray for those who run it, that God may guide them in their daily decisions. Pray for the Churches, that they may lead people to God.

Walk with God

ALONE with none but thee, my God,
I journey on my way.
What need I fear when thou art near,
O King of night and day?
More safe am I within thy hand
Than if a host did round me stand.

ST COLUMBA

🍂 Take a long walk, talking to God along the way.

H E didn't exactly accuse God of inefficiency, but when he prayed his voice was loud and angry, like that of a dissatisfied guest in a carelessly managed hotel.

CLARENCE DAY

   ❧ How often do you find yourself complaining to God that he is not working in the way you want him to? Remind yourself that God is the creator of the universe and therefore knows what's best for you.

Be aweful.

Love all God's creatures

HE prayeth well, who loveth well
Both man and bird and beast.
SAMUEL TAYLOR COLERIDGE,
The Rime of the Ancient Mariner

Pray for all God's creatures, knowing that he loves
and cares for all of them.

THE true worshippers are those who worship God in spirit and in truth. All who believe their prayers will not be heard sin upon the left hand of this scripture in that they go far astray with their unbelief. But those who set times, places, measures and limits for God sin upon the right hand and come too close with their tempting of God. So God has forbidden us to err from his commandment on either the left or the right, that is, either with unbelief or with tempting. Instead we are to come to God in simple faith, remaining on the straight road, trusting him and yet setting him no bounds.

MARTIN LUTHER, *Table Talk*

🐚 Have you ever set limits on God? If so, ask his forgiveness. Resolve not to do this again, but to be content that his timing and will are perfect.

Marvel at God's power

ETERNAL God,
 You are the power behind all things …
 Behind the energy of the atom,
 Behind the heat of a million suns.

Eternal God,
 You are the power behind all minds …
 Behind the ability to think and reason,
 Behind all understanding of the truth.

Eternal God,
 You are the power behind the cross of Christ …
 Behind the weakness, the torture and the death,
 Behind unconquerable love.

Eternal power,
 We worship and adore you.
More Contemporary Prayers, edited by Caryl Micklem

🐚 Marvel at the power of God. Reflect upon how one so powerful came to earth as a baby. What does this tell you about God?

Pick flowers

ONE should gather a little nosegay of devotion. My meaning is as follows: Those who have been walking in a beautiful garden do not leave it willingly without taking with them four or five flowers, in order to inhale their perfume and carry them about during the day; even so, when we have considered some mystery in meditation, we should choose one or two or three points in which we have found most relish, and which are specially proper to our advancement, in order to remember them throughout the day, and to inhale their perfume spiritually.

ST FRANCIS DE SALES,
Introduction to the Devout Life

❧ At the end of your next prayer time, jot down three things God revealed to you, and remind yourself of them throughout the day.

See work as prayer

TO work is to pray.

BENEDICTINE MOTTO

❧ Think about ways in which your work might be a prayer to God. Then, when you're next at work, take a moment out of your busy schedule to reflect on this.

I F Christ himself needed to retire from time to time to the mountain-top to pray, lesser men need not be ashamed to acknowledge that necessity.

B. H. STREETER, *Concerning Prayer*

🍃 Spend some time in prayerful solitude, and resolve to set aside time to do this regularly.

Be humorous

HUMOUR is a prelude to faith and laughter is the beginning of prayer.

<small>REINHOLD NIEBUHR,</small>
Discerning the Signs of the Times

🐾 The next time you find yourself laughing at something, praise God for the fun in life.

Cherish your friends

H ELP me, O God, to be a good and a true friend:
to be always loyal and never to let my friends down;
never to talk about them behind their backs in a way
   which I would not do before their faces;
never to betray a confidence or talk about the things
   about which I ought to be silent;
always ready to share everything I have;
to be as true to my friends as I would wish them to be
   to me.
This I ask for the sake of him who is the greatest and
   truest of all friends.

WILLIAM BARCLAY

🐾 Pray for one of your closest friends – then give
them a surprise bunch of flowers or box of chocolates
to show how much you appreciate their friendship.

Don't feel you have to explain

PRAYER should be short, without giving God Almighty reasons why he should grant this or that. He knows what is best for us.

JOHN SELDEN

🙙 Talk to God about your concerns, without explaining why you feel you need certain things. Be brief, and listen to his response.

Whatsoever we beg of God, let us also work for it.

JEREMY TAYLOR

What would you most like from God? Without ceasing to pray for it, think of ways in which you can work towards it.

Talk to God in the kitchen

THE time of business does not with me differ from the
time of prayer, and in the noise and clatter of my
kitchen, while several persons are at the same time
calling for different things, I possess God in as great
tranquillity as if I were upon my knees at the blessed
sacrament.

BROTHER LAWRENCE

🕭 The next time you're cooking or washing up,
spend the time talking to God.

Watch creation's praise

MAY none of God's wonderful works keep silence,
night or morning.
Bright stars, high mountains, the depths of the seas,
sources of rushing rivers:
may all these break into song as we sing
to Father, Son and Holy Spirit.
May all the angels in the heavens reply: Amen! Amen!
Amen!
Power, praise, honour, eternal glory to God the only
giver of grace.
Amen! Amen! Amen!

THIRD-CENTURY HYMN

🕭 Watch God's creation singing its praises to God –
and join in with it.

Seek spiritual direction

HUMILITY and docile acceptance of sound advice are very necessary in the life of prayer. Though spiritual direction may not be necessary in the ordinary Christian life, and though a monk may be able to get along to some extent without it (many have to!), it becomes a moral necessity for anyone who is trying to deepen his or her life of prayer.

THOMAS MERTON, *Contemplative Prayer*

🐾 Does your church offer spiritual direction? If so, arrange to see a spiritual director. If not, read books or sermons by a devotional writer who you would most like to have as your spiritual director.

Create a prayer chart

INTERCESSION also names the leaders of mankind in statecraft, medicine, learning, art and religion; the needy of the world; our friends at work or play, and our loved ones. A sense of responsibility may prompt us to prepare a chart of intercession, so that day by day we may enter earnestly into the needs of the world, and not forget nor fail anyone who closely depends upon our prayers.

GEORGE A. BUTTRICK, *Prayer*

🦋 Start to keep a list or chart of people you need to pray for. Divide them into seven groups, and pray for one group every day of the week.

Love your enemies

BUT I say to you that listen: love your enemies, do good to those who hate you, bless those who curse you, pray for those who abuse you. If anyone strikes you on the right cheek, offer the other also; and from anyone who takes away your coat do not withhold even your shirt. Give to everyone who begs from you; and if anyone takes away your goods, do not ask for them again. Do to others as you would have them do to you.
LUKE 6:27–31

🐌 Today, ask God to bless someone you dislike or who dislikes you. Ask him to bless their personal life, their relationships, their working life. Ask him to help them with any problems they may have. Finally, pray that God's forgiveness will inflame you and pour out from you towards them.

Don't worry if you don't understand

PRAYER is a little like an automobile; you do not
have to understand everything about its inner workings
for it to get you somewhere.

RICHARD FOSTER, *Devotional Classics*

🖎 Don't worry if you don't understand the mysteries
of prayer. Just pray – God is listening.

Pray on the street

Our Lord did not say it was wrong to pray in the corners of the street, but he did say it was wrong to be 'seen of men'.

OSWALD CHAMBERS, *Christian Discipline Vol. II*

🐾 As you walk along the street today, pray without anyone noticing. Pray for what you see around you and for the people you see.

Look to the light

GLORY be to you for the visible light: the sun's radiance, the flame of fire; day and night, evening and morning.

LANCELOT ANDREWES, *Private Devotions*

Look out of the window and thank God for giving light to the world, both literally and spiritually.

Check your diary

I F your Bible is the first great aid to prayer, your diary will be the second. Commit to him in the morning the details of the day which lies before you, and in the evening run through the day again, confessing the sins you have committed, giving thanks for the blessings you have received and praying for the people you have met.

JOHN STOTT, *Basic Christianity*

🦩 Check your diary for forthcoming appointments and anniversaries. Pray about the appointments and for those who are celebrating birthdays or anniversaries.

Just do it!

To quench thirst it is necessary to drink. Reading books about it only makes it worse.

JEAN-PIERRE DE CAUSSADE,
The Sacrament of the Present Moment

If you want to pray – just do it!

Be changed through prayer

PRAYER can never be prayer unless it leads to love.
DELIA SMITH, *A Journey into God*

❧ Look back over your prayer life. How has it changed you? Are you more devoted to God, do you have more love for all his people? If not, ask God where you are going wrong.

Identify with written prayers

WE all know God in different ways, therefore every person's prayers are unique. No one shares quite the same relationship with God. That is why personal, extempore prayer is so important. But we also have much in common as human beings, so written prayers can reflect the desires of many hearts, just as great love poetry expresses the feelings of thousands who are in love.

MARY BATCHELOR, *The Lion Prayer Collection*

Choose a written prayer with which you most identify. Pray that prayer for yourself.

Pray for young people

LORD, I pray for the young people of our world today. Give them a vision which is your vision so that there may be peace and justice in our world.

ANTHEA DOVE, *Out of the Ordinary*

Pray for the young people of the world. Then consider what you can do, on a practical level, for the young people in your area and resolve to act on your thoughts.

O God our Saviour, who willest that all men should be saved and come to the knowledge of the truth, prosper, we pray thee, our brethren who labour in distant lands. Protect them in all perils by land and sea, support them in loneliness and in the hour of trial; give them grace to bear faithful witness unto thee, and endue them with burning zeal and love, that they may turn to righteousness and finally obtain a crown of glory; through Jesus Christ.

Scottish Book of Common Prayer (1912)

🔖 Choose a missionary society whose work you can support through prayer and donations. Ask them for a list of missionaries to pray for.

Pray for your whole self

GOD cares as much about the body as he does the soul, as much about the emotions as he does the spirit. The redemption that is in Jesus is total, involving every aspect of the person – body, soul, will, mind, emotions, spirit.

RICHARD FOSTER, *Prayer*

🐚 Is there any aspect of yourself you have neglected to pray for? Pray about it now, knowing that God is interested in all of you.

WHAT I say I don't feel
What I feel I don't show
What I show isn't real
What is real, Lord – I don't know.

I don't know why every time
I find a new love I end up destroying it.
I don't know why I'm
So freaky-minded, I keep on kind of enjoying it –
Why I drift off to sleep
With pledges of resolve again,
Then along comes the day
And suddenly they dissolve again –
I don't know …

What I need I don't have
What I have I don't own
What I own I don't want
What I want, Lord, I don't know.

LEONARD BERNSTEIN, *Mass*

❧ Be totally honest with God about how you *really* feel about yourself, your life, the world and your faith.

Pray for pressing needs

WE should pray by fixing our mind upon some pressing need, desiring it with all earnestness, and then exercise faith and confidence toward God in the matter, never doubting that we have been heard.

MARTIN LUTHER, *Table Talk*

What need is uppermost on your mind right now? Talk to God about it and then rest assured that he has listened.

Meet God in the morning

'IF you fix your daily Quiet Time at night it will be backward-looking. If you fix it in the morning it will be forward-looking,' said one great prayer warrior. He did not mean, of course, that we need not pray in the evening, but the main thrust of our prayer-time should be at the freshest part of the day, when our minds are clear and we can give our attention more firmly to the task of prayer.

SELWYN HUGHES, *CWR Prayer Diary*

❧ Resolve to meet God first thing every morning this week.

Make your work hours glorious

IT seems now to me that yonder plowman could be like Calixto Sanidad, when he was a lonesome and mistreated plowboy, 'with my eyes on the furrow, and my hands on the lines, but my thoughts on God'. The millions at looms and lathes could make the hours glorious. Some hour spent by some night-watchman might be the most glorious ever lived on earth.

FRANK LAUBACH, *Letters by a Modern Mystic*

🔖 Today, pray throughout a mundane task. Consider continuing this practice on a regular basis.

Close your eyes

To be there before you, Lord, that's all.
To shut the eyes of my body,
To shut the eyes of my soul,
And be still and silent,
To expose myself to you who are there, exposed to me.
To be there before you, the Eternal Presence.

MICHEL QUOIST

Close your eyes, block out your circumstances,
and meet God.

Don't blot out the blessings

A lecturer to a group of businessmen displayed a sheet of white paper on which was one blot. He asked what they saw. All answered, 'A blot'. The test was unfair: it invited the wrong answer. Nevertheless, there is an ingratitude in human nature by which we notice the black disfigurement and forget the widespread mercy.

GEORGE A. BUTTRICK, *Prayer*

🔖 Think about the 'blots' in your own life at present. Are they really so enormous compared with all the blessings you have?

WE should never make prayer too complicated. We are prone to do so once we understand that prayer is something we must learn.

RICHARD FOSTER, *A Celebration of Discipline*

🐾 Don't complicate prayer – for yourself or for others. Be direct and straightforward, leaving out all unnecessary detail.

Don't trust your feelings

WE should not, however, judge the value of our meditation by 'how we feel'. A hard and apparently fruitless meditation may in fact be much more valuable than one that is easy, happy, enlightened, and apparently a big success.

THOMAS MERTON, *Contemplative Prayer*

🐚 Spend some time in prayer and meditation – and then ignore your feelings about it.

DEAR Lord Jesus, we shall have this day only once; before it is gone, help us to do all the good we can, so that today is not a wasted day.

STEPHEN GRELLET

🔖 Ask God to help you see every day as 1,440 minutes of opportunity to serve him.

Pray constantly

WE have the idea that prayer is for special times, but we have to put on the armour of God for the continual practice of prayer, so that any struggling onslaught of the powers of darkness cannot touch the position of prayer.

OSWALD CHAMBERS, *If Ye Shall Ask*

❧ Today, try to pray regularly throughout the day rather than at one set time.

CONFESSION to those we have wronged is sometimes, not always, wise: there are circumstances in
which such confession would spread and aggravate the
hurt. But confession to God, whom we have deeply
wronged, is always wise: he has understanding and
love.

GEORGE A. BUTTRICK, *Prayer*

🐾 Confess your sins to God. Ask for discernment in
recognizing when confessing to a person you have
wronged is the right thing to do.

Learn on the job

THERE is no better way to learn about prayer than by praying.
RICHARD FOSTER, *Devotional Classics*

🥢 Settle down to pray straight away and make a note of anything you learned from it – about prayer, about God, about your faith, your relationships, yourself.

MOST problems in contemporary churches can be explained by the fact that most members have not yet decided to follow Christ.

DALLAS WILLARD, *The Spirit of the Disciplines*

🐚 Pray for the conversion of those members of your church who have not yet committed themselves to Jesus.

Be cheerful at work

FATHER, give us endurance and cheerfulness as we face the tasks of everyday life. Each of us knows the monotony or difficulty of our own daily work. Help us not to look enviously at others' jobs but to shoulder our own work cheerfully as doing it for you.

MARY BATCHELOR

❧ The next time you have to complete a mundane task at work or at home, make an effort to be cheerful. Pray that your cheerfulness may uplift those around you carrying out similar mundane tasks.

Learn from the disciples

ONE day the disciples said to Jesus Christ, 'Lord, teach us to pray.' It was the Holy Spirit who inspired them to make this request. The Holy Spirit convinced them of their inability to pray in their own strength, and he moved their hearts to draw near to Jesus Christ as the only Master who could teach them how they ought to pray. It was then that Jesus taught them the Lord's Prayer.

There is no Christian who is not in the same case as the disciples. Every Christian ought to say to the Saviour as humbly as they, 'Lord, teach us to pray.'

JEAN-NICHOLAS GROU, *How To Pray*

Thank God for the example of the disciples. Ask him to show you how to pray, as he showed them.

Pray for local workers

GRANT unto farmers good seasons. Grant unto the fishermen good weather. Grant unto the tradesmen a desire not to compete with one another. Grant unto all merchants to pursue their business with lawful integrity.

LANCELOT ANDREWES, *Private Devotions*

🕭 Think of the main industries and professions in your area. Pray for all who work in them.

FOR when we hold up the life of another before God, when we expose it to God's love, when we pray for its release from drowsiness, for the quickening of its inner health, for the power to throw off a destructive habit, for the restoration of its free and vital relationship with its fellows, for its strength to resist temptation, for its courage to continue against sharp opposition – only then do we sense what it means to share in God's work, in his concern; only then do the walls that separate us from others go down and we sense that we are at bottom all knit together in a great and intimate family.

DOUGLAS V. STEERE, *Prayer and Worship*

Spend some time in prayer for another person. Pray about their love and work, their relationships, their sorrows and their joys. Understand something of God's concern for that person.

Intercede

INTERCEDING does not mean reminding God of things he has forgotten to do. It is placing ourselves at the heart of a troubled situation.

ANTHONY BLOOM

❧ Pray for a country currently in the news because of war, famine or other tragic reasons. Pray for the victims, the country's leaders, the aid workers.

Acknowledgements

My thanks are due to the following people who either directly or indirectly helped me to compile this book: members of the Endowed Mission Hall in Rowley Regis who kindly lent me various spiritual classics; Bruce Clift and Jane Foulkes for introducing me to other useful books; my parents Vera and Richard Round and then-fiancé (now my husband), Grant Filleul, who gave me space in which to work; and Christine Smith, editorial director of Marshall Pickering, for her help and encouragement, and for commissioning me in the first place.

The acknowledgements pages constitute an extension of the copyright pages.

Abingdon Press, for excerpts from the following:
1. *Private Devotions* by Lancelot Andrewes, taken from *The Fellowship of the Saints*, by Thomas S. Kepler, copyright 1947 by Stone & Peers, copyright renewal 1976 by Florence Tennant Kepler.
2. *Prayer* by George A. Buttrick.

Friends United Press, for excerpts from *Prayer and Worship* by Douglas V. Steere.

HarperCollins, for excerpts from the following:
1. *The Sacrament of the Present Moment* by Jean-Pierre

de Caussade.

2. *Christian Discipline* Vol. II by Oswald Chambers.
3. *If Ye Shall Ask* by Oswald Chambers.
4. *A Testament of Devotion* by Thomas Kelly.
5. *Making All Things New* by Henri Nouwen.
6. *The Growing Up Pains of Adrian Plass*, by Adrian Plass.
7. *The Spirit of the Disciplines* by Dallas Willard.

HarperCollins *Religious*, Melbourne, Australia, for excerpts from *Common Prayer Collection* by Michael Leunig.

Hodder and Stoughton, for excerpts from the following:
1. *Celebration of Discipline* by Richard Foster.
2. *Devotional Classics* by Richard Foster.
3. *Prayer* by Richard Foster.
4. *Listening to God* by Joyce Huggett.
5. *A Journey into God* by Delia Smith.

IVP, for an excerpt from *Basic Christianity* by John Stott.

Lion Publishing for excepts from the following:
1. *The Lion Prayer Collection* by Mary Batchelor.
2. *What's the Point?* by Norman Warren.

Macmillan Publishing Company and Oxford University Press, for excerpts from *A Diary of Private Prayer* by John Baillie.

Mowbray, for excerpts from *Further Everyday Prayers.*

New Reader's Press, for excerpts from *Letters by a Modern Mystic* by Frank Laubach.

SCM Press, for excerpts from *More Contemporary Prayers* edited by Caryl Micklem.

Sheed and Ward, for an excerpt from *Prayers of Life* by Michel Quoist.

Triangle, for an excerpt from *The Badge of Glory* by David Adam.

All Bible quotations are taken from the NRSV.